Scholastic Success With

TESTS
READING
WORKBOOK
GRADE 2

From the Editors of *Scholastic News*

D0910751

SCHOLASTIC
PROFESSIONAL BOOKS

New York ⊚ **Toronto** ⊚ **London** ⊚ **Auckland** ⊚ **Sydney**
Mexico City ⊚ **New Delhi** ⊚ **Hong Kong** ⊚ **Buenos Aires**

The Scholastic Success With Tests: Reading series is designed to help you help students succeed on standardized tests. In this workbook for second grade, the 11 four-page tests are culled from the Basic Skills Practice Tests provided twice a year to *Scholastic News Edition 2* subscribers, with some new and revised material. By familiarizing children with the skills, language, and formats they will encounter on state and national tests, like the Terra Nova, ITBS, CTBS, and MAT, these practice tests will boost confidence and help raise scores.

Each practice test contains at least five of the following components:

- **Phonic Analyis: Consonants**, designed to check students' knowledge of consonants, consonant blends, and digraphs in initial and final positions.
- **Phonic Analyis: Vowels**, designed to check students' knowledge of long-vowel sounds and diphthongs.
- **Phonemic Awareness**, designed to check students' awareness of distinct sounds and syllables. (See the **Answer Key** on pages 47-48 for sentences to dictate to students in this section.)
- **Dictation**, designed to check students' ability to recall and spell words that frequently appear in second-grade reading materials. (See the **Answer Key** on page 47-48 for words to dictate to students in this section.)
- **Vocabulary: Picture-Word Match**, designed to check students' ability to attach meaning to print and to identify decodable second-grade words.
- **High-Frequency Word Match**, designed to check students' ability to recognize words commonly found in second-grade reading materials. (See the **Answer Key** on pages 47-48 for words to dictate to students in this section.)
- **Word-Match Dictation**, designed to check students' ability to distinguish between homophones and other confusing words. (See the **Answer Key** on pages 47-48 for sentences to dictate to students in this section.)
- **Synonyms**, designed to check students' knowledge of synonyms.
- **Antonyms**, designed to check students' knowledge of antonyms.
- **Grammar, Usage, and Mechanics**, designed to check students' ability to use correct punctuation, capitalization, and verb tenses.
- **Story Comprehension**, designed to check students' ability to comprehend a reading passage.
- **Reading a Graph**, designed to check a students' ability to read graphs.

Suggestions for Administering the Tests

Treat these practice tests as confidence-building exercises. Help students understand that this practice will help them become more skilled and ultimately perform better when they have to take "real" tests later on.

Give students the sense of taking standardized tests when they work on these practice tests. Do the sample questions together and go over the directions for each section, making sure that students understand them. After each test, review it together to reinforce specific skills.

Analyzing Test Results

The **Answer Key** for the practice tests is provided on pages 47-48. As you review each practice test together, help the children understand the reasoning behind the correct choices. Encourage students to share their own strategies as well. Note any common weaknesses for an immediate mini-lesson or future follow-up lessons.

Cover design by Maria Lilja • Cover art by Victoria Raymond
ISBN 0-439-42573-5
Copyright © 2002 by Scholastic Inc. All rights reserved. Printed in the USA.
11 12   40   08

Reading Skills Practice Test I

A. PHONIC ANALYSIS: CONSONANTS

Look at each picture.
Write the missing letter or letters on the blank line.

Sample	1.	2.
_____at	_____indow	_____eese
3.	**4.**	**5.**
_____ip	_____og	_____amp
6.	**7.**	**8.**
ha_____	tee_____	tru_____

B. DICTATION

Write the word after your teacher says it.

Sample

_____

1. _____

_____

2. _____

3. _____

_____

C. VOCABULARY: PICTURE-WORD MATCH

Fill in the bubble next to the word that names each picture.

Sample	1.	2.
O girl O gift O giraffe	O life O leaf O leak	O ball O barn O bull
3. O main O mine O moon	**4.** O box O boy O boil	**5.** O mice O mound O mouse

D. HIGH-FREQUENCY WORD MATCH

Fill in the bubble next to the word your teacher says out loud.

Sample	1.	2.
O the O this O thick	O of O over O or	O fun O from O fresh
3. O has O had O have	**4.** O when O where O which	**5.** O throw O through O thing

E. GRAMMAR, USAGE, AND MECHANICS

Read each sentence. Fill in the bubble next to the word or words that best fit in the blank.

Sample

_____ ran up the hill.

- O he
- O He
- O He's

1. Did you take that book _____
   - O home.
   - O home
   - O home?

2. We _____ outside all day.
   - O plays
   - O played
   - O playing

3. _____ is our teacher this year.
   - O mrs smith
   - O Mrs Smith
   - O Mrs. Smith

4. _____ is in my class.
   - O Maria
   - O maria
   - O MARIA

5. I _____ have any homework last week.
   - O didnt
   - O didnt'
   - O didn't

F. STORY COMPREHENSION

Read the story. Then answer each question.
Fill in the bubble next to the best answer.

Frogs lay their eggs in ponds. The eggs grow. Slowly, they turn into tadpoles. The tadpoles grow and change. They become frogs.

The frogs hop. They can hop onto land. They can even hop onto rocks in the pond. Frogs stay near the pond. There they can get water. They can also catch bugs to eat.

1. Where do frogs lay their eggs?
- O on lily pads
- O in ponds
- O under rocks

2. What is a good title (name) for this story?
- O Farm Animals
- O Kittens Play
- O Frogs

3. What does a tadpole become?
- O a fish
- O a frog
- O an egg

4. What do frogs eat?
- O rocks
- O bugs
- O hay

Reading Skills Practice Test 2

A. PHONIC ANALYSIS: CONSONANTS

Look at each picture.

Write the missing letter or letters on the blank line.

Sample	1.	2.
_____ar	_____ock	_____ain
3.	**4.**	**5.**
ne _____	_____at	fi _____

B. PHONIC ANALYSIS: VOWELS

Look at each picture.

Write the missing letter or letters on the blank line.

Sample	1.	2.
ch _____ se	br _____ m	c _____ t
3.	**4.**	**5.**
m _____ se	thr _____	b _____ k _____

C. DICTATION

Write the word after your teacher says it.

Sample

_____

- - - - - - - - - - - - - - - - - -

_____   **1.**_____

_____

- - - - - - - - - - - - - - - - - -   - - - - - - - - - - - - - - - - - -

2._____   **3.**_____

D. HIGH-FREQUENCY WORD MATCH

Fill in the bubble next to the word your teacher says out loud.

Sample	**1.**	**2.**
O when O where O which	O over O of O off	O every O vest O very
3.	**4.**	**5.**
O knew O know O knot	O cook O coat O could	O some O something O summer

E. GRAMMAR, USAGE, AND MECHANICS

Read each sentence. Fill in the bubble next to the word or words that best fit in the blank.

Sample _____ plays in the park.
- O he
- O He
- O He's

1. Did you see that _____
- O star.
- O star
- O star?

2. We _____ in the yard.
- O runs
- O run
- O running

3. _____ is my neighbor.
- O mr smith
- O Mr Smith
- O Mr. Smith

4. She moved to _____
- O New York.
- O new york.
- O NEW YORK.

5. He _____ come to my house today.
- O cant
- O cant'
- O can't

6. Watch _____
- O out.
- O out!
- O out?

7. The dog _____ the cat.
- O chased
- O chasing
- O chase

8. _____ is nice.
- O dr hamilton
- O Dr Hamilton
- O Dr. Hamilton

9. We went to _____
- O texas.
- O TEXAS.
- O Texas.

F. STORY COMPREHENSION

Read the story. Then answer each question.
Fill in the bubble next to the best answer.

A whale is a very big animal. Whales live in the sea. Some whales swim with each other. They travel in large groups, called pods. They swim around, looking for food.

Whales feed on sea life. Some whales eat plants. Other whales have teeth and can eat seals and small fish.

Whales must stay wet all the time. However, they also must come to the top of the sea to breathe. When a whale leaps out of the water to catch a breath of air, it is an amazing sight.

1. What are pods?
   O   whale food
   O   groups of whales
   O   sea animals

2. What is a good title (name) for this story?
   O   The Sea
   O   Fish
   O   Whales

3. What must all whales do?
   O   eat seals and fish
   O   spend time on land
   O   stay wet

4. Why do whales sometimes jump out of the water?
   O   to warm up
   O   to get air
   O   to catch fish

Reading Skills Practice Test 3

A. PHONIC ANALYSIS: CONSONANTS

Look at each picture.

Write the missing letter or letters on the blank line.

Sample	1.	2.
_____ar	_____ed	_____ock

3.	4.	5.
_____apes	ha_____	too_____

B. PHONIC ANALYSIS: VOWELS

Look at each picture.

Write the missing letter or letters on the line.

Sample	1.	2.
b_____t	h_____se	f_____t

3.	4.	5.
sp_____n	tr_____n	k_____t_____

C. Dictation

Write the word after your teacher says it.

Sample

_____   _____
- - - - - - - - - - - - - - -   **1.** - - - - - - - - - - - - - - - - -
_____   _____

_____   _____
2. - - - - - - - - - - - - - -   **3.** - - - - - - - - - - - - - - - -
_____   _____

D. High-Frequency Word Match

Fill in the bubble next to the word your teacher says out loud.

Sample	**1.**	**2.**
O where O then O there	O above O about O away	O shall O ship O should
3.	**4.**	**5.**
O those O this O though	O know O knew O now	O every O something O everything

E. Grammar, Usage, and Mechanics

Read each sentence. Fill in the bubble next to the word or words that best fit in the blank.

Sample _____ walk to school.
- ○ they
- ○ she
- ○ They

1. I _____ my bike in the park.
   - ○ rides
   - ○ ride
   - ○ riding

2. Can you lift this _____
   - ○ box?
   - ○ box
   - ○ box.

3. My friend's name is _____
   - ○ peter Jones.
   - ○ Peter Jones.
   - ○ Peter Jones

4. We live in _____
   - ○ maine.
   - ○ Maine.
   - ○ MAINE.

5. Be _____
   - ○ careful!
   - ○ careful.
   - ○ careful?

6. I _____ want to play.
   - ○ dont'
   - ○ dont
   - ○ don't

7. We _____ at his house.
   - ○ playing
   - ○ played
   - ○ plays

8. _____ on her way home.
   - ○ she's
   - ○ She
   - ○ She's

9. Our family doctor is _____.
   - ○ dr. Smith
   - ○ Dr. Smith
   - ○ Dr Smith

F. STORY COMPREHENSION

Read the story. Then answer each question.
Fill in the bubble next to the best answer.

A tornado is a kind of wind storm. The winds can be very strong. A tornado is shaped like a funnel. Sometimes, a tornado is called a "twister."

Most tornadoes take place in April, May, or June. They usually happen on hot days.

A tornado does not last long. But it can wreck everything in its path! When a tornado comes, the safest place to be is below ground. That's why people often go to their basements before a tornado comes.

1. What is a good title (name) for this story?

   O Storms
   O Tornadoes
   O Wind

2. What is a twister?

   O a basement
   O a tornado
   O a hard rain

3. When do tornadoes usually happen?

   O only in June
   O in winter
   O on hot days

4. Why do people go to their basements before a tornado comes?

   O to be safe
   O to watch the storm
   O to play games

Reading Skills Practice Test 4

A. PHONIC ANALYSIS: CONSONANTS

Look at each picture.

Write the missing letter or letters on the blank line.

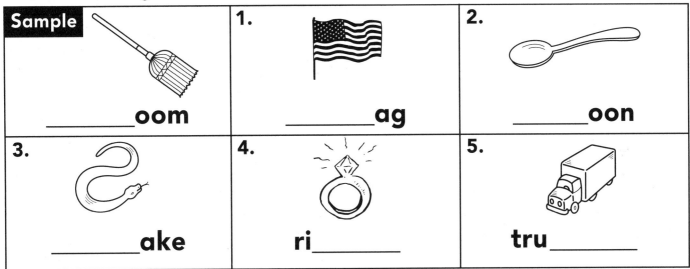

Sample
_____oom

1.
_____ag

2.
_____oon

3.
_____ake

4.
ri_____

5.
tru_____

B. PHONIC ANALYSIS: VOWELS

Look at each picture.

Write the missing letter or letters on the line.

Sample
b_____k_____

1.
c_____t

2.
c_____k_____

3.
l_____f

4.
r_____n

5.
c_____ch

C. PHONEMIC AWARENESS

Write the number of syllables in each word your teacher says out loud.

Sample _____   **1.** _____   **2.** _____

3. _____   **4.** _____   **5.** _____

D. HIGH-FREQUENCY WORD MATCH

Fill in the bubble next to the word your teacher says out loud.

Sample	**1.**	**2.**
O when O how O who	O after O afraid O often	O skate O school O shore
3. O between O because O beneath	**4.** O might O mice O mitten	**5.** O knew O now O know

E. GRAMMAR, USAGE, AND MECHANICS

Read each sentence. Fill in the bubble next to the word or words that best complete each sentence.

Sample

_____ walk to school.
- O She
- O We
- O they

1. The boys _____ their pictures.
- O colors
- O coloring
- O color

2. Yesterday, I _____ with my friend.
- O played
- O play
- O plays

3. What is in your _____
- O bag?
- O bag.
- O bag

4. Look _____
- O out
- O out!
- O out?

5. My dog _____ run.
- O won't
- O wont
- O wont'

6. _____ going to the fair.
- O She
- O shes'
- O She's

7. My mother _____ me a new coat next week.
- O will buy
- O buy
- O bought

8. I went on a trip to _____
- O florida.
- O FLORIDA
- O Florida.

9. _____ gave me a checkup.
- O dr. Lee
- O Dr. Lee
- O Dr Lee

F. Story Comprehension

Read the story. Then answer each question.
Fill in the bubble next to the best answer.

Tigers are the world's biggest cats. Most tigers are bigger than lions. A tiger's body can be as long as a car. A tiger can even weigh as much as two adult people!

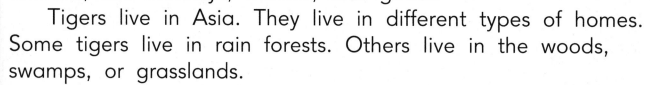

Tigers are good hunters. Why? They are good at jumping. They are fast. They can see well in the dark. When tigers hunt at night, they surprise other animals. A tiger's favorite foods are deer and wild pigs. They also eat other animals, like monkeys, buffalo, and goats.

Tigers live in Asia. They live in different types of homes. Some tigers live in rain forests. Others live in the woods, swamps, or grasslands.

1. What is a good title (name) for this story?

- O Animals
- O Cats
- O Tigers

2. What animals do tigers often eat?

- O deer and wild pigs
- O pigs and dogs
- O birds and lions

3. Where do tigers live?

- O Africa
- O Mexico
- O Asia

4. Write a sentence telling why tigers are good hunters.

_____

_____

_____

Reading Skills Practice Test 5

A. PHONIC ANALYSIS: CONSONANTS

Look at each picture.
Write the missing letter or letters on the blank line.

Sample	1.	2.
_____ee	_____air	_____ane
3.	4.	5.
_____ake	ne_____	fi_____

B. PHONIC ANALYSIS: VOWELS

Look at each picture.
Write the missing letter or letters on the blank line.

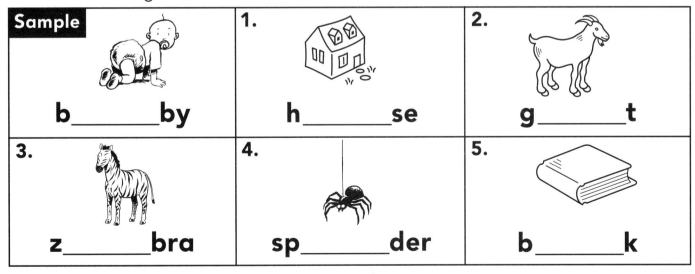

Sample	1.	2.
b_____by	h_____se	g_____t
3.	4.	5.
z_____bra	sp_____der	b_____k

C. DICTATION

Write the word after your teacher says it.

Sample

_____   _____
- - - - - - - - - - - -   - - - - - - - - - - - -
_____   **1.**_____

_____   _____
- - - - - - - - - - - -   - - - - - - - - - - - -
2._____   **3.**_____

D. HIGH-FREQUENCY WORD MATCH

Fill in the bubble next to the word your teacher says out loud.

Sample	**1.**	**2.**
O when O why O which	O over O or O off	O every O vest O very
3.	**4.**	**5.**
O knew O know O knot	O will O weed O would	O tugging O together O teacher

E. GRAMMAR, USAGE, AND MECHANICS

Read each sentence. Fill in the bubble next to the word or words that best fit in the blank.

Sample _____ ran in the park.
- ○ she
- ○ She
- ○ She's

1. Did you read that _____
- ○ book.
- ○ Book.
- ○ book?

2. We _____ in the lake.
- ○ swims
- ○ swam
- ○ swimming

3. _____ is my dentist.
- ○ dr bell
- ○ Dr Bell
- ○ Dr. Bell

4. She lives in _____
- ○ Centerville.
- ○ centerville.
- ○ CENTERVILLE.

5. He _____ be at the soccer game.
- ○ wont
- ○ wont'
- ○ won't

6. Watch _____
- ○ out.
- ○ out!
- ○ out?

7. The rabbit _____ to the carrot.
- ○ hoped
- ○ hopping
- ○ hopped

8. _____ drove the school bus.
- ○ mrs campbell
- ○ Mrs Campbell
- ○ Mrs. Campbell

9. We took a trip to _____
- ○ new york.
- ○ NEW YORK.
- ○ New York.

10. I _____ go to the park.
- ○ couldnt
- ○ couldn't
- ○ couldnt'

F. Story Comprehension

Read the story. Then answer each question. Fill in the bubble next to the best answer.

Many animals have claws. Claws are like your fingernails. Animal claws can be long or short. Most claws are very sharp.

Claws have many uses. Birds have claws called talons. These claws help them to hold on to things and to catch their food. Bears have claws on their large paws. They use their claws to get food and to climb up trees. Cats have claws that help them to climb and hold on to things. Cats like to scratch with their claws. Scratching keeps their claws sharp.

1. What are talons?
- O cat claws
- O bird claws
- O bear claws

2. What is a good title (name) for this story?
- O Birds
- O Climbing
- O Claws

3. How do animals use claws?
- O to hold on to things
- O to write in the sand
- O to swim in the ocean

4. Which animal has claws?
- O fish
- O bear
- O snake

Reading Skills Practice Test 6

A. PHONIC ANALYSIS: CONSONANTS

Look at each picture.

Write the missing letter or letters on the blank line.

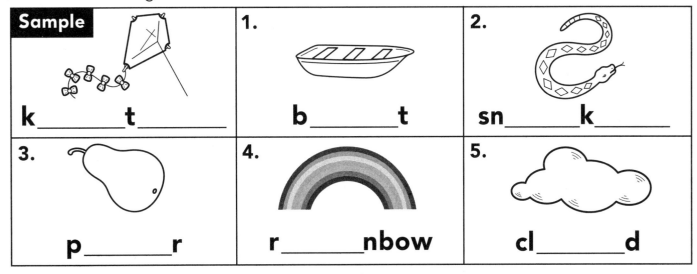

Sample	1.	2.
_____ar	_____apes	_____ide
3.	**4.**	**5.**
_____anch	ha_____	clo_____

B. PHONIC ANALYSIS: VOWELS

Look at each picture.

Write the missing letter or letters on the line.

Sample	1.	2.
k_____t	b_____t	sn_____k_____
3.	**4.**	**5.**
p_____r	r_____nbow	cl_____d

C. PHONEMIC AWARENESS

Write the number of syllables in each word your teacher says out loud.

Sample _____   **1.** _____   **2.** _____

3. _____   **4.** _____   **5.** _____

D. GRAMMAR, USAGE, AND MECHANICS

Read each sentence. Fill in the bubble next to the word or words that best complete each sentence.

Sample _____ rides a horse.
- ○ she
- ○ She
- ○ We

1. The children _____ soccer.
- ○ play
- ○ plays
- ○ playing

2. Last night, we _____ a great movie.
- ○ watch
- ○ watching
- ○ watched

3. Which story is _____
- ○ yours!
- ○ yours.
- ○ yours?

4. That frog _____ jump.
- ○ wont
- ○ wont'
- ○ won't

5. _____ going to the zoo.
- ○ He's
- ○ He
- ○ Hes'

6. My book _____ in the mail tomorrow.
- ○ came
- ○ come
- ○ will come

7. _____ read a story to us.
- ○ ms. Jones
- ○ Ms Jones
- ○ Ms. Jones

E. STORY COMPREHENSION

Read the story. Then answer each question.
Fill in the bubble next to the best answer.

A baby elephant grows up with its family, or **herd**. A herd is made up of mothers, sisters, cousins, and aunts.

The herd takes care of the **calf**, or baby elephant, in many ways. A mother stands over her calf to keep it safe from danger and the hot sun. An aunt helps the calf keep up when the herd is walking. When an enemy is near, the adult elephants stand in front of the calf. Then, the oldest female fans out her ears to look big and angry. The herd doesn't want anything to happen to the calf.

1. What is a good title (name) for this story?

O Mother Elephants

O Elephant Herds

O Adult Elephants

2. What is a calf?

O a baby elephant

O the oldest elephant

O an elephant family

3. When an elephant fans out its ears, it looks _____.

O big and funny

O small and angry

O big and angry

4. Write a sentence telling one way the herd helps the baby.

_____

_____

_____

F. Story Comprehension

Read the story. Then answer each question.
Fill in the bubble next to the best answer.

> Chinese New Year is the most important Chinese holiday. It celebrates the end of one year and the beginning of a new year. The holiday falls in January or February and lasts for 15 days.
>
> People do many things to get ready for Chinese New Year. They clean and decorate their homes. They buy flowers and new clothes.
>
> When the holiday starts, people visit with family and friends. They gather for a big feast. They also go to parades, where they see dancers, drummers, and colorful dragons.

1. What is a good title (name) for this story?

  ○ Dragons
  ○ China
  ○ Chinese New Year

2. Chinese New Year lasts for how long?

  ○ 24 days
  ○ 15 days
  ○ one year

3. People get ready for the holiday by _____.

  ○ cleaning their homes
  ○ dancing
  ○ going to parades

4. Write a sentence telling some ways that people celebrate Chinese New Year. _____

_____

_____

Reading Skills Practice Test 7

A. PHONIC ANALYSIS: CONSONANTS

Look at each picture.
Write the missing letter or letters on the blank line.

Sample _____ider	**1.** wat_____	**2.** _____an
3. _____ant	**4.** lo_____	**5.** bo_____

B. PHONIC ANALYSIS: VOWELS

Look at each picture.
Write the missing letter or letters on the line.

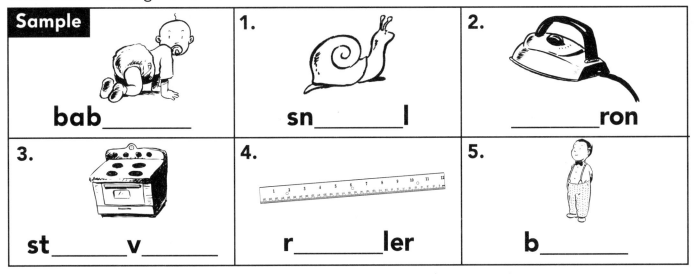

Sample bab_____	**1.** sn_____l	**2.** _____ron
3. st_____v_____	**4.** r_____ler	**5.** b_____

C. PHONEMIC AWARENESS

Write the number of syllables in each word your teacher says out loud.

Sample _____   **1.** _____   **2.** _____

3. _____   **4.** _____   **5.** _____

D. GRAMMAR, USAGE, AND MECHANICS

Read each sentence. Fill in the bubble next to the word or words that best complete each sentence.

Sample _____ live in a city.
- O they
- O They
- O He

1. The farm animals _____ grain.
- O eating
- O eats
- O eat

2. Today, we will _____ the dog a bath.
- O gived
- O giving
- O give

3. Ouch! A bee stung _____
- O Me.
- O me?
- O me!

4. I _____ swim in the deep water yet.
- O cant
- O can't
- O cant'

5. _____ going to the library.
- O She's
- O Shes
- O Shes'

6. My aunt _____ me to the movies tomorrow.
- O take
- O took
- O will take

7. _____ fixed my bike.
- O Mr. Smith
- O mr. Smith
- O Mr Smith

E. STORY COMPREHENSION

Read the story. Then answer each question.
Fill in the bubble next to the best answer.

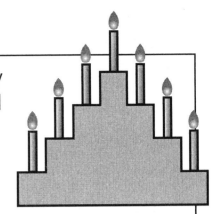

Kwanzaa is a holiday celebrated by many people who have African **ancestors.** The word **ancestors** means family who lived before you —like your great, great, great grandparents. Kwanzaa celebrates families and sticking together. It always lasts for seven days, beginning on December 26th and ending on January 1st.

People do many things to celebrate Kwanzaa. They dress in special clothes and decorate their homes with fruits and vegetables. Families and friends get together for big meals. Children get gifts, like books and toys.

One of the most important parts of Kwanzaa is lighting candles in the **kinara.** The kinara is a special candleholder with seven candles. People who celebrate Kwanzaa light one candle each night.

1. What is a good title (name) for this story?
O Kwanzaa
O Children Get Gifts
O Ancestors

2. Kwanzaa lasts for how many days?
O 1
O 7
O 26

3. A kinara is a
O kind of clothing
O kind of food
O kind of candleholder

4. Write a sentence telling some ways that people celebrate Kwanzaa.

_____

_____

F. Reading a Graph

Look at the graph. Then answer each question. Fill in the bubble next to the best answer.

Lost Teeth
Hardy School, Grade 2

Number of Teeth Lost

equals one student.

---

1. What is this graph about?
- ○ which students like teeth
- ○ Hardy School
- ○ how many teeth students have lost

2. How many students have lost six teeth?
- ○ 2 students
- ○ 3 students
- ○ 4 students

3. What's the largest number of teeth that any student has lost?
- ○ 4
- ○ 7
- ○ 20

4. How many students have lost five teeth?
- ○ 0
- ○ 1
- ○ 2

Reading Skills Practice Test 8

A. PHONIC ANALYSIS: CONSONANTS

Look at each picture.

Write the missing letter or letters on the blank line.

Sample	1.	2.
_____ar	_____ale	_____ower

3.	4.	5.
_____ree	de_____	_____ebra

B. PHONIC ANALYSIS: VOWELS

Look at each picture.

Write the missing letters on the blank line.

Sample	1.	2.
f_____t	wh_____l	cl_____d

3.	4.	5.
r_____dio	br_____d	p_____

C. GRAMMAR, USAGE, AND MECHANICS

Read each sentence. Fill in the bubble next to the word or words that best fit in the blank.

Sample

_____ go to the park.
- O we
- O We
- O We've

1. Can she run in the _____
- O race.
- O race
- O race?

2. They _____ baseball.
- O play
- O plays
- O playing

3. _____ is my teacher.
- O mrs miller
- O Mrs Miller
- O Mrs. Miller

4. She went on a trip to _____.
- O boston
- O Boston
- O BOSTON

5. He _____ drive the car.
- O couldnt
- O couldnt'
- O couldn't

6. _____ There is a fire!
- O Help.
- O Help!
- O Help?

7. My aunt lives in _____.
- O Dallas, Texas
- O dallas, texas
- O Dallas Texas

8. _____ eat out," said Mom.
- O let's
- O Let's
- O "Let's

9. The children can _____ around the track.
- O ran
- O runs
- O run

D. STORY COMPREHENSION

Read the story. Then answer each question.
Fill in the bubble next to the best answer.

We get many useful things from trees. Wood comes from trees. The wood can be used to make houses, desks, and chairs. Rubber comes from trees. Rubber is used to make balls and boots. We also get fruit and nuts from trees. Birds and other animals like these tree treats, too.

Trees can be helpful. Some medicines are made from tree bark. These medicines help sick people get well. Trees also give us shade on a sunny day. Many animals make their homes in trees. Birds build nests on tree branches. Owls, foxes, and other animals can live in tree holes.

1. What is a good title (name) for this story?
- O Growing Trees
- O Animals and Trees
- O Trees Are Important

2. What do people <u>and</u> animals use from trees?
- O desks
- O food
- O rubber

3. What animal can make its home in a tree?
- O the fox
- O the horse
- O the elephant

4. What other thing might you make from a tree?
- O a car
- O a baseball bat
- O a computer

E. READING A GRAPH

Look at the graph. Then answer each question.
Fill in the bubble next to the best answer.

Favorite Sports
Mrs. Smith's Class, Grade 2

number of students	baseball	football	soccer	gymnastics	skating
10			■		
9			■		
8			■	■	
7			■	■	
6			■	■	
5	■		■	■	■
4	■		■	■	■
3	■		■	■	■
2	■	■	■	■	■
1	■	■	■	■	■

1. What is this graph about?
- O soccer and basketball
- O what sports kids like best
- O Mrs. Green's class

2. Which sport is liked by the most students?
- O soccer
- O skating
- O gymnastics

3. How many students like baseball best?
- O 2
- O 5
- O 7

4. Which 2 sports are liked by the same number of students?
- O baseball and soccer
- O gymnastics and soccer
- O skating and baseball

Reading Skills Practice Test 9

A. PHONIC ANALYSIS: CONSONANTS

Look at each picture.

Write the missing letter or letters on the blank line.

Sample	1.	2.
_____arn	_____eese	fi_____
3.	**4.**	**5.**
te_____	_____ush	_____own

B. PHONIC ANALYSIS: VOWELS

Look at each picture.

Write the missing letter or letters on the line.

Sample	1.	2.
m_____n	h_____se	f_____t
3.	**4.**	**5.**
p_____r	fl_____	c_____n

C. GRAMMAR, USAGE, AND MECHANICS

Read each sentence. Fill in the bubble next to the word or words that best fit in the blank.

Sample

_____ race down the hill.
- O We
- O we
- O She

1. May I go to the _____
- O store.
- O store?
- O Store?

2. _____ plays football every day.
- O he
- O He
- O They

3. I saw _____ at the park.
- O Mrs Walker
- O mrs. walker
- O Mrs. Walker

4. I will visit my uncle in _____
- O March.
- O march.
- O MARCH.

5. _____ You hit the ball hard.
- O Wow
- O Wow!
- O Wow.

6. I _____ run as fast as Sam.
- O cant
- O cant'
- O can't

7. _____ on my way," said Jane.
- O I'm
- O "Im
- O "I'm

8. Yesterday, we _____ our bikes.
- O ride
- O rode
- O riding

9. We will soon move to _____
- O Kansas.
- O Kansas
- O kansas.

D. Story Comprehension

Read the story. Then answer each question.
Fill in the bubble next to the best answer.

Most people go to sleep at night. So do many animals. But a few animals sleep most of the day. Then they stay up all night. These animals can use their senses to get around in the dark.

Owls, skunks, and moths all stay up at night. The owl has very large eyes that can see in the dark. Both the skunk and the moth have a very strong sense of smell. They can smell other animals from very far away.

Why do some animals stay up all night? Sometimes, it's because nighttime is the best time to hunt. In hot places, animals can stay cooler at night. There are many reasons animals come out at night.

1. What is a good title (name) for this story?
- O Owls
- O Night Animals
- O Sleep

2. What do both skunks and moths have?
- O large eyes
- O a strong sense of smell
- O a bad smell

3. The owl's large eyes help it to
- O see in the dark.
- O see in the daytime.
- O sleep very well.

4. What might be another reason to stay up at night?
- O to get a suntan
- O to grow food
- O to hide from other animals

E. READING A GRAPH

Look at the graph. Then answer each question.
Fill in the bubble next to the best answer.

STUDENTS' FAVORITE COLORS
Park School, Grade 2

COLORS	1	2	3	4	5	6	7	8	9	10
red	■	■	■	■	■	■				
blue	■	■	■	■	■	■	■	■	■	
yellow	■	■	■	■						
green	■	■	■	■	■	■				

NUMBER OF STUDENTS

---

1. What is this graph about?
- ○ how colors are made
- ○ what colors students like best
- ○ South School, Grade 2

2. How many students like red the best?
- ○ 7
- ○ 4
- ○ 6

3. Which two colors are liked by the same number of students?
- ○ red and blue
- ○ red and green
- ○ blue and green

4. How many more students like the color blue better than the color green?
- ○ 2
- ○ 3
- ○ 4

Reading Skills Practice Test 10

A. WORD-MATCH DICTATION

Fill in the bubble next to each word that fits in the sentence your teacher says out loud.

Sample	1.	2.
O two	O deer	O we're
O too	O dear	O were
O to	O den	O where
3.	**4.**	**5.**
O knife	O sent	O there
O night	O scent	O they're
O knight	O cent	O their

B. SYNONYMS

Fill in the bubble next to the word that means the **same** as the **bold** word.

Sample	1.	2.
big O small	**happy** O sad	**fast** O funny
O large	O shy	O quick
O skinny	O glad	O slow
3.	**4.**	**5.**
answer O respond	**brave** O scared	**mad** O furious
O ask	O proud	O smart
O tell	O fearless	O laugh

C. ANTONYMS

Fill in the bubble next to the word that means the **opposite** of the **bold** word.

Sample	1.	2.
day O school	**old** O young	**hot** O cold
O time	O age	O warm
O night	O long	O strange
3.	**4.**	**5.**
clean O nice	**tall** O high	**strong** O weak
O dirty	O smooth	O powerful
O run	O short	O wild

D. GRAMMAR, USAGE, AND MECHANICS

Read each sentence. Fill in the bubble next to the word or words that best fit in the blank.

Sample

The boy walked _____
- ◯ home
- ◯ home.
- ◯ home,

1. Where do you _____
- ◯ live!
- ◯ live
- ◯ live?

2. Maria and I play ____
- ◯ soccer.
- ◯ soccer?
- ◯ soccer

3. Our teacher is _____
- ◯ mr. lee.
- ◯ Mr. Lee.
- ◯ mr. Lee.

4. We will _____ a movie tomorrow.
- ◯ watch
- ◯ watched
- ◯ watches

5. Trish turned 8 years old on _____
- ◯ February, 22. 2000
- ◯ February 22, 2000.
- ◯ February 22. 2000

6. _____ is in the South.
- ◯ Texas
- ◯ texas
- ◯ TEXAS

7. Yesterday, my mom ____ me with my homework.
- ◯ helped
- ◯ helps
- ◯ helping

8. Owls ____ sleep at night.
- ◯ don't
- ◯ dont'
- ◯ dono't

9. Jake is _____ than Ed.
- ◯ more tall
- ◯ taller
- ◯ tallest

10. Is this _____ book?
- ◯ them
- ◯ us
- ◯ your

11. We went for a ride in _____ car.
- ◯ Mike's
- ◯ mike's
- ◯ Mike

E. STORY AND GRAPH COMPREHENSION

Read the story and look at the graph. Then answer each question. Fill in the bubble next to the best answer.

Watch out for tornadoes in spring! A tornado, or a twister, is a dangerous storm. Tornadoes form when air begins to spin under a thundercloud. The air whirls around very fast. It twists so fast that it can lift up a car or a tree.

Mr. Smith's second-grade class researched how many tornadoes hit their county in the last five years. Look at the graph to see what they found out.

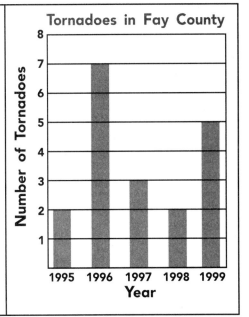

Tornadoes in Fay County

1. What is another name for a tornado?
   - O cloud
   - O hurricane
   - O twister

2. When do you think most tornadoes take place?
   - O spring
   - O summer
   - O winter

3. In which year did the most tornadoes hit Fay County?
   - O 1995
   - O 1996
   - O 1997

4. How many more tornadoes were there in 1999 than in 1998?
   - O 3
   - O 4
   - O 5

F. Story Comprehension

Read the story. Then answer each question.
Fill in the bubble next to the best answer.

Spiders are **carnivores**. That means that they eat other animals to survive. Spiders eat insects.

Different spiders have different ways to catch insects. A web weaver builds sticky webs to trap insects. A wandering hunter walks about in search of something to eat. When it sees an insect, it jumps on top of its prey. A tube dweller hides in the ground and waits for insects to come by. Then it springs up and catches its tasty meal.

Spiders help people by eating insects. How? Spiders eat insects that destroy farmers' crops. Spiders also eat insects that carry diseases. So if you see a spider, let it be!

1. What is a good title (name) for this story?
   O Wonderful Webs
   O Insects Everywhere
   O Hungry Spiders

2. A **carnivore** is an animal that eats other _____ .
   O animals
   O insects
   O plants

3. How do spiders help people?
   O They hide when people are near.
   O They don't eat animals.
   O They eat insects that destroy crops.

4. Write a sentence telling one or more ways a spider can catch its food.

   _____

   _____

Reading Skills Practice Test II

A. WORD-MATCH DICTATION

Fill in the bubble next to each word that fits in the sentence your teacher says out loud. Write the missing letters on the line.

Sample	1.	2.
O one O won O win	O said O sad O sand	O mad O made O mud
3. O pull O pill O pail	**4.** O tore O tear O tire	**5.** O hear O here O hair

B. SYNONYMS

Fill in the bubble next to the word that means the **same** as the **bold** word.

Sample	1.	2.
middle O center O side O front	**child** O kid O adult O smiled	**shut** O open O lock O close
3. **look** O hear O see O taste	**4.** **says** O tells O yells O plays	**5.** **done** O completed O behind O good

C. ANTONYMS

Fill in the bubble next to the word that means the **opposite** of the **bold** word.

Sample	1.	2.
many O few O a lot O money	**yours** O that O mine O those	**long** O tall O big O short
3. **quiet** O loud O shy O silent	**4.** **grow** O rise O shrink O flower	**5.** **more** O better O big O less

D. GRAMMAR, USAGE, AND MECHANICS

Read each sentence. Fill in the bubble next to the word or words that best fit in the blank.

Sample

It is time for _____
- ○ bed
- ○ bed.
- ○ bed,

1. Did you brush your _____
- ○ teeth?
- ○ teeth.
- ○ teeth

2. Pam and I played with _____
- ○ blocks
- ○ blocks.
- ○ Blocks.

3. School is over at _____
- ○ Three O'clock.
- ○ three o'clock
- ○ three o'clock.

4. Today I will ____ piano.
- ○ practice
- ○ practices
- ○ practicing

5. What _____ you want for your birthday?
- ○ does
- ○ do
- ○ Do

6. _____ is where the President lives.
- ○ Washington
- ○ washington
- ○ WASHINGTON

7. Will you _____ me on the swing?
- ○ pushed
- ○ pushing
- ○ push

8. I am ____ reading this book.
- ○ finish
- ○ finished
- ○ Finish

9. ____ can ride a horse.
- ○ She
- ○ she
- ○ she's

10. Jack's brother will turn 5 on _____.
- ○ October 28, 2002
- ○ october 28, 2002
- ○ October 29. 2002

11. _____ cat has kittens.
- ○ Tim's
- ○ Tims
- ○ tim's

E. Story Comprehension

Read the story. Then answer each question.
Fill in the bubble next to the best answer.

When you were born, you had 300 bones in your body! Why so many? They do many different jobs. Bones in your back, arms, and legs allow you to stand up and move around. Other bones protect your insides. Your skull, for example, is like a hard helmet for your brain. Your ribs protect your heart and lungs.

Did you know that bones are alive? They are made of hard stuff and tiny living cells, so small you need a microscope to see them. The living cells help your bones grow as you get older. If you break a bone, the living cells help heal it.

1. When you were born, you had _____ bones.
- O 100
- O 200
- O 300

2. Your skull protects your _____.
- O brain
- O arms
- O legs

3 What is in your bones that can help heal them?
- O ribs
- O microscope
- O living cells

4. A good title for this story is:
- O Babies
- O Legs
- O Your Bones

F. STORY COMPREHENSION

Read the story. Then answer each question.
Fill in the bubble next to the best answer.

> When astronauts go to work in space, they are too far away to come home each night. They have to live in space for a short time to do their work. But life in space is different from life on earth! The main reason is that there is less **gravity**. Gravity is the invisible force that holds everything—even you—to the earth. With less gravity, astronauts' feet don't stay on the ground, so they float instead of walk. It feels a bit like swimming. At night, astronauts sleep in sleeping bags strapped to the walls so they don't float around. To eat without pots and pans flying, astronauts have special foods like dried scrambled eggs. To get clean, astronauts rub soap and water on their bodies and sponge it off. That's because a shower would spray all over.

1. Why do astronauts have to live in space to do their work?
   - O They are lost.
   - O They are too far away to come home each night.
   - O They are floating.

2. The force that holds you to the earth is called _____.
   - O gravity
   - O astronaut
   - O eggs

3. One thing an astronaut has to do in space is:
   - O sleep in a sleeping bag strapped to the walls.
   - O eat candy.
   - O watch TV.

4. Write a sentence telling something about life in space.

_____

_____

Answer Key

TEST I

A. Phonic Analysis: Consonants
Sample: cat
1. window 2. geese
3. ship 4. dog 5. lamp
6. hat 7. teeth 8. truck

B. Dictation
Sample: slide
1. boat 2. under 3. come

C. Vocabulary: Picture-Word Match
Sample: girl
1. leaf 2. barn 3. moon
4. boy 5. mouse

D. High-Frequency Word Match
Sample: the
1. or 2. from 3. have
4. where 5. through

E. Grammar, Usage, and Mechanics
Sample: He ran up the hill.
1. Did you take that book **home?**
2. We **played** outside all day.
3. **Mrs. Smith** is our teacher this year.
4. **Maria** is in my class.
5. I **didn't** have any homework last week.

F. Story Comprehension
1. in ponds 2. Frogs
3. a frog 4. bugs

TEST 2

A. Phonic Analysis: Consonants
Sample: car
1. block 2. train 3. nest
4. bat 5. fish

B. Phonic Analysis: Vowels
Sample: cheese
1. broom 2. coat
3. mouse 4. three 5. bike

C. Dictation
Sample: rain
1. shake 2. is 3. some

D. High-Frequency Word Match
Sample: where
1. off 2. very 3. know
4. could 5. something

E. Grammar, Usage, and Mechanics
Sample: He plays in the park.
1. Did you see that **star?**
2. We **run** in the yard.
3. **Mr. Smith** is my neighbor.
4. She moved to **New York.**
5. He **can't** come to my house today.
6. Watch **out!**
7. The dog **chased** the cat.
8. **Dr. Hamilton** is nice.
9. We went to **Texas.**

F. Story Comprehension
1. groups of whales
2. Whales
3. stay wet
4. to get air

TEST 3

A. Phonic Analysis: Consonants
Sample: car
1. bed 2. clock 3. grapes
4. hand 5. tooth

B. Phonic Analysis: Vowels
Sample: boat
1. house 2. feet 3. spoon
4. train 5. kite

C. Dictation
Sample: like
1. math 2. what 3. could

D. High Frequency Word Match
Sample: there
1. about 2. should
3. those 4. knew
5. everything

E. Grammar, Usage, and Mechanics
Sample: They walk to school.
1. I **ride** my bike in the park.
2. Can you lift this **box?**
3. My friend's name is **Peter Jones.**
4. We live in **Maine.**
5. Be **careful!**
6. I **don't** want to play.
7. We **played** at his house.
8. **She's** on her way home.
9. Our family doctor is **Dr. Smith.**

F. Story Comprehension
1. Tornadoes 2. a tornado
3. on hot days 4. to be safe

TEST 4

A. Phonic Analysis: Consonants
Sample: broom
1. flag 2. spoon 3. snake
4. ring 5. truck

B. Phonic Analysis: Vowels
Sample: bike
1. coat 2. cake 3. leaf
4. rain 5. couch

C. Phonemic Awareness
Sample: pencil —2
1. tomato—3
2. map—1
3. information—4
4. bookmark—2
5. elephant—3

D. High-Frequency Word Match
Sample: who
1. after 2. school
3. because 4. might 5. know

E. Grammar, Usage, and Mechanics
Sample: We walk to school.
1. The boys **color** their pictures.
2. Yesterday, I **played** with my friend.
3. What is in your **bag?**
4. Look **out!**
5. My dog **won't** run.
6. **She's** going to the fair.
7. My mother **will buy** me a new coat next week.
8. I went on a trip to **Florida.**
9. **Dr. Lee** gave me a checkup.

F. Story Comprehension
1. Tigers
2. deer and wild pigs
3. Asia
4. Answers will vary

TEST 5

A. Phonic Analysis: Consonants
Sample: tree
1. chair 2. plane 3. snake
4. nest 5. fish

B. Phonic Analysis: Vowels
Sample: baby
1. house 2. goat 3. zebra
4. spider 5. book

B. Dictation
Sample: live
1. her 2. draw 3. book

D. High Frequency Word Match
1. which 2. off 3. every
4. knot 5. will 6. together

E. Grammar, Usage, and Mechanics
Sample: She ran in the park.
1. Did you read that **book?**
2. We **swam** in the lake.
3. **Dr. Bell** is my dentist.
4. She lives in **Centerville.**
5. He **won't** be at the soccer game.
6. Watch **out!**
7. The rabbit **hopped** to the carrot.
8. **Mrs. Campbell** drove the school bus.
9. We took a trip to **New York.**
10. I **couldn't** go to the park.

F. Story Comprehension
1. bird claws
2. Claws
3. to hold on to things
4. bear

TEST 6

A. Phonic Analysis: Consonants
Sample: star
1. grapes 2. slide 3. branch
4. hand 5. clock

B. Phonic Analysis: Vowels
Sample: kite
1. boat 2. snake 3. pear
4. rainbow 5. cloud

C. Phonemic Awareness
Sample: apple—2
1. soup—1
2. cartwheel—2
3. television—4
4. shirt—1
5. animals—3

D. Grammar, Usage, and Mechanics
Sample: She rides a horse.
1. The children **play** soccer.
2. Last night, we **watched** a great movie.
3. Which story is **yours?**
4. That frog **won't** jump.
5. **He's** going to the zoo.
6. My book **will come** in the mail tomorrow.
7. **Ms. Jones** read a story to us.

E. Story Comprehension
1. Elephant Herds
2. a baby elephant
3. big and angry
4. Answers will vary

F. Story Comprehension
1. Chinese New Year
2. 15 days
3. cleaning their homes
4. Answers will vary.

Test 7
A. Phonic Analysis: Consonants
Sample: spider
1. watch 2. swan
3. plant 4. lock 5. box

B. Phonic Analysis: Vowels
Sample: baby
1. snail 2. iron 3. stove
4. ruler 5. boy

C. Phonemic Awareness
Sample: paper—2
1. elephant—3
2. ice—1
3. information—4
4. president—3
5. apple—2

D. Grammar, Usage, and Mechanics
Sample: They live in a city.
1. The farm animals **eat** grain.
2. Today, we will **give** the dog a bath.
3. Ouch! A bee stung **me!**
4. I **can't** swim in the deep water yet.
5. **She's** going to the library.
6. My aunt **will take** me to the movies tomorrow.
7. **Mr. Smith** fixed my bike.

E. Story Comprehension
1. Kwanzaa
2. 7
3. kind of candleholder
4. Answers will vary.

F. Reading a Graph
1. how many teeth students have lost
2. 4 students
3. 7
4. 0

TEST 8
A. Phonic Analysis: Consonants
Sample: star
1. whale 2. flower
3. three 4. desk 5. zebra

B. Phonic Analysis: Vowels
Sample: foot
1. wheel 2. cloud 3. radio
4. bread 5. pie

C. Grammar, Usage, and Mechanics
Sample: We go to the park.
1. Can she run in the **race?**
2. They **play** baseball.
3. **Mrs. Miller** is my teacher.
4. She went on a trip to **Boston.**
5. He **couldn't** drive the car.
6. **Help!** There is a fire!
7. My aunt lives in **Dallas, Texas.**
8. **"Let's** eat out," said Mom.
9. The children can **run** around the track.

D. Story Comprehension
1. Trees Are Important
2. food
3. the fox
4. a baseball bat

E. Reading a Graph
1. what sports kids like best
2. soccer
3. 5
4. skating and baseball

TEST 9
A. Phonic Analysis: Consonants
Sample: yarn
1. cheese 2. fish 3. tent
4. brush 5. clown

B. Phonic Analysis: Vowels
Sample: moon
1. house 2. feet 3. pear
4. fly 5. coin

C. Grammar, Usage, and Mechanics
Sample: We race down the hill.
1. May I go to the **store?**
2. **He** plays football every day.
3. I saw **Mrs. Walker** at the park.
4. I will visit my grandma in **March.**
5. **Wow!** You hit the ball hard.
6. I **can't** run as fast as Sam.
7. **"I'm** on my way," said Jane.
8. Yesterday, we **rode** our bikes.
9. We will soon move to **Kansas.**

D. Story Comprehension
1. Night Animals
2. a strong sense of smell
3. see in the dark
4. to hide from other animals

E. Reading a Graph
1. what colors students like best
2. 6
3. red and green
4. 3

TEST 10
A. Word-Match Dictation
Sample: I know the way to the playground.
1. We saw a **deer** in the woods.
2. **Where** do you want to go?
3. We got home last **night.**
4. I **sent** the letter yesterday.
5. Tim and Anna got mud on **their** clothes.

B. Synonyms
Sample: large
1. glad 2. quick 3. respond
4. fearless 5. furious

C. Antonyms
Sample: night
1. young 2. cold 3. dirty
4. short 5. weak

D. Grammar, Usage, and Mechanics
Sample: The boy walked home.
1. Where do you **live?**
2. Maria and I play **soccer.**
3. Our teacher is **Mr. Lee.**
4. We will **watch** a movie tomorrow.
5. Trish turned 8 years old on **February 22, 2000.**
6. **Texas** is in the South.
7. Yesterday, my mom **helped** me with my homework.
8. Owls **don't** sleep at night.
9. Jake is **taller** than Ed.
10. Is this **your** book?
11. We went for a ride in **Mike's** car.

E. Story and Graph Comprehension
1. twister 2. spring
3. 1996 4. 3

F. Story Comprehension
1. Hungry Spiders
2. animals
3. They eat insects that destroy crops.
4. Answers will vary.

TEST II
A. Word Match Dictation
*Sample: Who **won** the game?*
1. We built a **sand** castle.
2. I got **mad** at my brother.
3. Fill the **pail** with water.
4. Don't **tear** your jacket!
5. Did you **hear** the news?

B. Synonyms
Sample: center
1. kid 2. close 3. see
4. tells 5. completed

C. Antonyms
Sample: few
1. mine 2. short 3. loud
4. shrink 5. less

D. Grammar, Usage, and Mechanics
*Sample: It is time for **bed.***
1. Did you brush your **teeth?**
2. Pam and I played with **blocks.**
3. School is over at **three o'clock.**
4. Today I will **practice** piano.
5. What **do** you want for your birthday?
6. **Washington** is where the President lives.
7. Will you **push** me on the swing?
8. I am **finished** reading this book.
9. **She** can ride a horse.
10. Jack's brother will turn 5 on **October 28th, 2002.**
11. **Tim's** cat has kittens.

E. Story Comprehension
1. 300 2. brain
3. living cells 4. Your Bones

F. Story Comprehension
1. They are too far away to come home each night.
2. gravity
3. sleep in a sleeping bag strapped to the walls.
4. Answers will vary.